THE MACHINERY OF SLEEP

THE MACHINERY OF SLEEP

PATRICK CAHILL

Sixteen Rivers Press

Published by Sixteen Rivers Press
P.O. Box 640663
San Francisco, CA 94164-0663
www.sixteenrivers.org

LCCN: 2019948919
ISBN: 9781939639219

Cover Photo by Brendan Cahill
Design by Brendan Cahill

In memory of
Vickie Cahill

Contents

One

Two

Three

Four

Five

ONE

————————————————————
————————————————
————

*Let us call desire a kingdom
and naïveté the root of all being.*

—Dante Di Stefano,
"The 45th Psalm"

Another Air

Light
remember
its silver entered that wood
surface you rubbed with your thumb.

Later a hawk
rose against a deepening blue
absence of light.
Charmed particles

of inattention
whose tracings you want
some other sense to describe.
An error in the light of each

microcosmic event.
Figures in another air.

Cauchemar

Some invisible thing
lifted him up
off the bed
and threw him upward
into the terror

Brief Time

In one of her self-
portraits
Frida Kahlo translates
her shattered spine
into a fluted
column
of broken stone
ten years
before her death
ars longa
vita brevis
Seneca's translation
of Hippocrates
but in the original
art is the art
of medicine
and *life* this brief
poor allotment
given those
who hope to master
a most difficult art

Writing

Chinese is a beautiful language
signatures in snow

What is the character for *character*

      The dancer rose
that night from the floor
mistaken for one

Once he floated above a stair
and someone said
Why is he there

      A beautiful language, English
The *gombeen* man was a usurer
An example of prose

The Irish is lovely
extinguished among syllables of speech
Repeat it in English

      rain bitten

      weapons are common

      snow blossom

A nice language, invisible, others
The distance in verb

Now snow fills the pass above
the character for *memory*
Petals fall the color of jade
feathers the carved
heron or tern

Say *snow*   *gombeen* man
Say *jade*   winter rain
Translate *dance*

Hurricane Coast

Our kayak entered
Dutchman's Creek
followed the arrow (red) and black
gradations on the compass face
spinning and still

the white bird's feet
were yellow in the tree

Our diligent work
against the current's resistance
pure opium

Remembered now
the woman with the jeweled tooth
her rite of dubious authenticity

Water poured
from blade to wrist
from there to waist
and swamped our shell

when we were here or were we there

Alcohol illuminated
our neural streams
as periwinkles
measured the depth

a white bird's legs
trailed black in the sky

but we weren't as fortunate

that antebellum river port
its brackish mouth
overexposed in bioluminescent light

The panorama of our expedition
unscrolling across the simmering wash
altered our story's destination

we never were a beginning here

Mist drifted our vision

and in the Book
of Insect Migrations
we mapped our way

Portrait of the Artist as an Old Man

Humans
insects
suns

a girl in Rabat
her shadow blown

back from the sea
descending

eastward
after her shadow

into the dusk

time and grace

from these he'd inferred
a mockingbird

that whistled
and trilled the night

Re mem ber?

I remember her. Rather I remember a memory of her, a street in Rabat, a young woman, Moroccan, a narrow street down to the river, ocean or river, down to the water. A boy perhaps, was it a boy, androgynous, bringing coconuts down to a dock, splitting their shells. Rabat, or somewhere south on the coast. Another coast. A coast perhaps on the south of Spain. A Spanish girl down a narrow street in Cádiz, down to a gulf, the Gulf of Cádiz. *Was she beautiful?* The girl or the gulf? *The girl, was she beautiful?* I don't remember. *Her face?* How could I possibly remember her face? Hers or his, the androgynous boy. You remember the memory of a girl in Cádiz, Cádiz or Rabat, a girl or a boy, a narrow street, an impression of water. Coconuts spilling watery milk. A coast of Arabic aspect, Arabic façades adjoining it. Fractured shells, saltwater or funk—a river's funk, it rationed the air. A memory of memory's watery dissolves. This much I remember.

the flax field

        is blue
the ink that describes
           this field
of flowers
    is too

Shostakovich

for Aidan
after Su-Mei Tse's "Mistelpartition"

A moving row of poplars, leafless images across a wall. Their irresistible invisible road beneath our feet. Borderland. The monotony of equinox to solstice, solstice to summer's solitude, fabric of our gaze. A cello's measured solicitude compels the trees and our regard. Random lights flash their incantations, a code of little explosions among the leafless branches, layered over an image of winter air, our winter's distant present. A bluing sky's blue illusion—music's invention.

Cannonball Adderley, Jazz Workshop, 1959

Dmitri lifts his Russian hands bearlike into the hunger and begins to applaud, even though he hasn't moved to the beat of the music. Dmitri's motionless body conjugates its rhythms at play now in a metaphor of extended arms and moving hands.

Corpus: the body of men and animals, at rest and in motion one evening in 1959.

For Brendan

after Louis Zukofsky

to lift you then

into the swing

insula

sanctorum

the trees invading

whatever air

they became

when you

not two then

looked at one

and told

yourself its name

the garden

"look at the flowers," the child says
opening an anatomy book

The Dragon in the House

He looks back into the moon:
again the field he dreamt as a child
under its light,
and crossed toward the fence whose timbers
seemed to draw light up from the ground.

The dragon in the house he dreams
remembers the language even the child
crossing this field
no longer knows,
though he sang it once.

The door opens out of the light
that falls across him
onto the path, and stepping in,
into daylight,
he enters a garden.
The dragon lifts its head from the ground
as scales tremble,
unfolding into the leaves they become
and branches above.

A dragonfly darts
and glistens near the tree.
It frightens him,
even though he senses the music
its wings move to,

transforming them,
this apple blossom
falling through the light
it holds.

sea array

within each persimmon
    a starfish
imprints
    a self-impression

Abundance

under a current of black and yellow bees blue clusters
of ceanothus vibrate.   let the current etch its
confusions.   let the breath measure its aroma.   let
the soil darken its profusion.

These

Apples fall

into what

bruises

pulp and skin become

this earth around

rain clouds

the mountains

off whose contours birds deflect

catch the light there

and turn

to snow and vanish

changing

the wind our wrists hold

the moment these

become in us

inventing a space

whose margins

the trees

illuminate

TWO

_____

_____

_____

When I return to my studio from the night before, oftentimes things have either dis-appeared or something has appeared from out of nowhere.

—Jeannie Motherwell

the passage

he thought he was going to a city   going toward a city then

the landscape he navigated an index of memory and loss

hidden selves and memory's loss   leaves unfolded   tiny

green eyeless birds consuming the trees' branches   yet they cast

a maze on the air   a city between its coastline and wind-infested

space   a space spread out before him   a tide's salty currents

containing a shore   as thick as his blood a new moon turning

birds abandoned their web-shaped insignias in the mud   an

alphabet of puzzling dichotomies   a city he thought he was

going toward   inhabited among unwarranted consolations

a new moon's imprisoned light   hot-weather rain birds   the

road dissolving behind him   a city beside an ocean   a

distance   an opening up

To Persia and the Park Beyond

An incision crosses your heart. Lenticular clouds. The witch's cap. His features emerged from the philosophical delirium of the furnace. Your skirt a shade of rust, you wore a large red feather in a large black hat. *Amator* to amateur, or lover. You slid into third and leveled him again with your lips. You lack all calibration, either full on or off. Their wings spread between each breath, they glide on the thermals. At Diamond and Bosworth the 52. That or 40 below in the interior, your face against a confluence of optimism and ice. Your double deceived the assassin but ended her double's career. While you await the 52 to Persia and beyond. The hornet in the sonnet. The arsenic in the apple seed. Their feathers forming wings in the blood. *The harder they come.* And on the thermals they translate your knowing in their flight.

Weather Report

A flute over the river. A saxophone over the waste. I feel your walk in my walk, your pulse a beam of blue air across a window's diagonal. The nonstop repetition of a synthesizer's single note. Disintegrating sheets of blood fall through the water. Flickering patterns of light translate the floating text. *I will not send you into the darkness alone.* Although he did, of necessity. A blood slick just beneath her reflection ringing the glass. His weapon's "negligent discharge" opened a bright hole in his thigh. Someone boning kippers and someone dropped her knickers. Neon letters throb an emergency. Light a cigarette and it will go away. Extinguish the cigarette and only the music remains. Weather report. The atmospherics before the dance. I hear your voice in my voice, see not with but through your eyes. A massive translucent wave and inside its glassy curve a dolphin speeding its length.

I Don't Know What

The seasons picked up speed. Snowdrifts bent the fences. Telephone poles strung out the white miles of wind. Wind blew the sunlight. The gorgeous rain.

Draw an ellipse, spin it, then add a cloud of stars. Cosmic grit. Bacteria capture the earth's magnetic field. Migrate. As do we. *Do not drive at night do not take bullets guns or drugs.* We're out of flowers in English. Conscripted Latin is next. A brain atlas proposed for the mouse. Was it his fault? Was it ours? At every opportunity repeat the words: *Salt marsh harvest mouse. Salt march harvest mouth. Malt harsh marvest south.*

The dog with the thirst. A still life passes in a car. Always a clue. Cloud mechanics. Your face lost against the light. An apocalyptic goat plus an apoplectic owner. So sleepy he couldn't get to the end of the phrase. A word with a thousand meanings, the same meaning in each of a thousand words. Porcupines float. Wind blew her hair into the next county. More than you've ever been able to imagine. A corpse of a different choler. You never know what to expect of the young. *Besame besame mucho.* Kiss me a lot. You leave a lot. To be desired. And, it works. You've turned to salt again, babe.

Drift Prairie

Killdeer, our noisy country plover, cries its name as it hurries ahead, drags its broken unbroken performer's wing. Hatchlings? Watch your step. Against the black furrows a flurry of late stubborn snow, just before a prairie wind. Coteau des Prairies. An indirect expression of a direct impression. *The purpose of life*, he wrote. To follow the sentient disjunctive sentence into the noise, that stratus of birds, encrypted clues? Horses would help, their calculated lines against a middle-distant plowed disorder. Insect bother, cattail clutter. The slough seeping under us, it spoiled us then. Surface arias' vernal ice. These lakes bowls of glacial melt, glacier's pothole ghosts.

Badlands

Your liquid selves displacing the arid there   Twenty traces in twenty
towns   Your lover gone you fill the space with his photograph   The
picture arouses an intimacy the lover had not   You touch yourself
and feel the heat entering your fingertips   The blue of the Badlands
and just as intense   Your touch   *so what*   The music
scattered   *well you needn't*   *peace piece*   Night lightning and
under its violet circuitry your Badlands graph the night   You whet a
bone to make a knife   You conjure sleep to dream a knight   His
slow metallic gestures glint in the light   *Les mauvaises terres à*
traverser   *mako sica*   a convalescence from butte to butte   Cheat
medicine   Striations of its buried life   The Badlands you've just
begun to cross

Dark Druid of the Sídhe

The machinery of sleep deceived us. Scar City, a scarcity. Your day in the Sídhe one hundred contagious years. Nightshade. Above your breasts Cyrillic notations. You left the life, bound your words with yellow thread. An inhabited life, a resistance. Under a shotgun blast of stars, crawl space of the Sídhe. Your dark druid, twilight, scalpel, his drug. A small pendant, flakes of black and turquoise above your breasts. Threaded wire crosshatched the glass through which. Encroaching thin shoots and leaves thinned the sun. Laminar flow silkened a riverbed. Scar City, spirit haunt, insomnia, Druidville. Rivers of the Sídhe. A spherical pendant, flakes of unrecovered light. Turquoise and black his whispered seductions. The scar tissue beneath his song.

The Staring Girl

The staring girl arched over the counter. Motionless. Her mouth slightly open. A drop curtain rises, shudders, drops. Afterimage. The starlight of Ellington's voice arrives from 1954. Rain then hail clattering off the skylight. They took to the stage in a year of regrets. The staring girl's silhouette forms an arc above her cup of coffee. My insect fantasies, your sharpened horns. You like scumbled edges, you like bleeding into, the blurry line, the unfocused figure. So do I. Charcoal under the thumb, a smear of pearl. Her arc a comma between her inner amazement and mine. The hail finds its patterns hidden in the wind. An omen we've failed to articulate. The Starlight Lounge of 1961. We haven't yet stopped staring at her.

Woman with Dog

The dog sitting between her knees, his back to her, facing the aisle that separates us, the Church streetcar once again carrying us north. Blind, she runs the tips of her fingers over his eyes, then brings her hand, clouded with the dog's odor, up to her nose and breathes in the hour's scent. She touches his coat lightly then, around and under his collar, brushing against its metal links. Again she lifts her fingers up to her nose and breathes in, the dog passive, contemplative even, under her touch, indifferent to our passage, the lifting fog.

A Ghost in the Reflection

He enters the shop, doubled in its reflection off to the right. He doesn't know the room is an illusion, doesn't recognize the person watching him in the other room. He turns and passes the glass case with its confections, then steps aside to pass the person he doesn't know in the other room, the other who also steps aside to block his way. An irritated smirk distorts his face. He reaches out, touches the offered fingertips, now glassy and cold. The other smiles, refuses to move. Irritated, he turns away and prepares to leave, then sick with recognition, glances back.

THREE

There where the story and desire begin.

Pluto

Let me tell you a story, the sea-lion woman said. A dark blue fluid twisted down the polished surface of a metal bowl miles above the earth. Pluto moved into Scorpio's house and unpacked catastrophe. States failed.

Your vow of silence so difficult to evaluate. It's so. Silent. Save for that hammering just in back of you. Let's tie a vein inside your wrist, work the knot up your arm with finger and thumb.

Let me tell you a story, the she-lion woman said. Pluto minor walks into Scorpio's house, suitcase in tow, and opens it. Numerous catastrophic events. States fail. A blue morpho's blue wings reduced to mulch.

A man with a stubbled rectangular jaw is swept away. An honorable man, despite a drinking problem. And several misdemeanors. And one regrettable incident at the newt preserve and mud baths. Swept away in a hurricane.

Pluto still in residence in Scorpio's or someone's house. Pluto the rock. Pluto iced. The hammering wind. The hammering wind.

Doctor of Illusion

He was pursued. Pursued by the furies. They hid in the granite's sparkling seams, the warp of the trees. The voices passive in their pursuit. They came with their guns. The taste of a flower he couldn't place at the back of his mouth. The red dots of laser light adrift on his chest. Was it only the angle the language made visible? Whenever he turned? A Brownian movement of lethal intent.

She sneezed and it was New Year's Eve. At midnight she sneezed. The hole in the ticket window made a target of her face. Piano chords moved along the sidewalk. But it was only a circular hole in the glass. The concrete only sparkled and sang. Rain blew off the trees and scattered their dots of light.

A confusion now in the house. Was he innocent? Wasn't he yet equipped to equivocate?

They hid in the evening's insects. They hid in the shimmer of insect wings. Their red eyes adrift on his vest. Was there a doctor of illusion in the house?

Welt Detektiv

after William Kentridge's Five Themes *art exhibit*

He viewed his shell—an insect's?—a necessary adjustment. Also the extra legs. Insects, six. Spiders, eight. Five legs. Three. Mechanical. But then who was counting? His transformation of transportation. His life had become an endless surveillance loop. Their dark figures drag themselves across a screen. Shoulder their shapeless burdens. Spread wings melt into a blackened abstraction. His mind had learned to control the implement inside his head, activate the music that scored his day. Newsprint scrolled across the bridge of his nose. Their ragged shapes, black against the white light, stuttering from left to right across the screen. If only they had dared a supposition, there'd be a trace. An underground narrative stream surfaces, wet with expectation, then disappears. What does a *welt detektiv* detect? The torn edges of print widen crossing his face. Music floods the margins of his brain. Think, he thinks. Think down the volume, thought select a different score. But will he detect the cartoon bomb, its black sphere and sparkling wick, under the prostrate figure just ahead of us? Before the real explosion?

Frottage

Perpendicular hunger. She finishes chewing and runs her tongue across the front enamel of her teeth. They leave an impression. Fades like us into the obscurity of letters. Cocaine warms the Queen's veins. The King half clothed. The Queen in her queenly things. *The more clothing the more crime,* the King says, brushing against her. A quantum event. A five-dimensional blueprint quantifies the castle's maze. Six-sided crystals texture the coliseum. Re-pencil the parterre. *What's with all the numbers?* the Queen says, unraveling within the maze. The coliseum unmapped in the snow. The Queen rubs against the King, leaves an impression, begins to sing. *Fear water, fear water . . . That's it,* says the King. *Let's doll the place up.* She runs her tongue along the bottom edge of her teeth. *What's hunger?* she says. The King comes close. Friction.

The Language of Burial

Up in the wires a finch with its melodious song, that harsh note at the end of it. So like everything *we* do. Your graveyard for words—what grows there now? Phacelia and wood mint, or sow thistle and storksbill? How many did you bury yesterday? Fiddlesticks, porkpie hat, gee-whilikers, portmanteau? You know I'll miss porkpie hat and portmanteau. A cat in the sack—feline in a paper bag? musician in bed? Solo, or with a guest? Her voice held the note as I left the café, its paper cups and coffee beans.

Bar stools in a wavering line, not unlike the drunks who'll soon line up on them. Shall we will we join them? You carry your list wherever you go. Light and yet it weighs down your shoulder bag, lowers your left shoulder with its fragile weight. Now and then you take it out and broadcast its ruined remains, although your shoulder doesn't snap back. We just can't take you places, anymore.

~~Addendum~~

Those buried words, or soon to be. Light a candle, sing a verse of plainsong. Augustine did in the Isle of Thanet. That feeling of elation, and hopelessness. What will we do without ~~babushka~~? OK Frost quit ~~lollygagging~~ and mend the wall. Even though the stones won't stick. I will miss our ~~free-for-alls~~. Ditto ~~boogaloo~~. Though ~~ditto~~? No. Every metaphor at some stage of decay. The soap smells of cleaning fluid, the flowers draw flies. Our parsley has liquefied in its plastic bag. Let's don our ~~homburgs~~, ~~sashay~~ on into town, do the ~~tarantella~~, before it's too late. Let's take apart our ~~Uzis~~, throw a ~~temper tantrum~~, move into a ~~yurt~~. The pavement choppy ahead of us. No graphite in the ~~pencil~~, no ~~ink~~ in the well. The keys silent. The program frozen. I know I'll miss redacted. I will miss ~~delete~~—

Q's world (MIA)

Shawn occupies three bodies now   George in the condominium

     Johnny at the corner store   Shawn where he was by the

door   the coroner can't identify the body Shawn has left behind

     George and Johnny across the floor   Shawn and

     George still at the store   missing in action   MIA   I've

talked to Shawn I've followed George in the condominium

     saw a body at the corner store   the coroner knows that

someone is missing in action   missing a body   MIA

     whoever it is I can't find George   I can't find Johnny I

don't know Shawn in someone's body   where he was then by

     the door   I can't find him or anyone else within the ambit of

his body   can't find anyone's missing body   lost at

     the corner   I can't find the store   whose body is

lying on someone's floor   who's walking the condominium

     who's closing the door

Q's world (under the mountain)

a sword, you said   flame on beaten metal   a sword under

the mountain   you trace the body's outline   reanimated

    the body gone   a pooling bereft of soul   crows to the

south   the curve of a lip   this slurry of sounds into a silver

microphone   words you've heard   reanimated   spilling

out of a mouth now   concentric pooling under the mountain's

    contiguous air   its thickening   as crows swarm   her

outline a blur of words   their black feathers reflected   they

swarm from the south   merge with their reflections   recede

    as they lift up   their images one with the blackening pool

    words of blood spill from a silver microphone   the sword

under the mountain   flame on metal   you trace the body's

outline   its pooling circles concentric   her soul loose

her words adrift

Days Like This

The jacaranda's lavender petals fell through the night and fell through the day. Hadn't they removed the tools and the bodies yet? She let him talk, she imagined, for 30, 40 minutes to her sleeping phone. She steps out into the lavender drifts. The air muted, humid, slows the hours of her acceleration. The black phoebe spreads its wings and fans its tail in a dusty patch of sunlight. Its brown feathered edges remind her of. Among a red profusion of climbing bracts, clusters of eyes. Although the reverse is also true. She begins to paint the portrait of a dog. This has happened before. Paints instead a spider skittering into abstraction beyond the frame. There where the story and desire begin.

Word Thief

In the dim and artificial light of a winter evening, a shadow and its grounded leaf simulate a lizard, or did the shadow only imply a leaf? In a place she left. Her radiant streams. Cordelia, her cat. More oil than rain spilling prisms across the mud, a dim and diamond winter light. Blue hair transits a window. Blue heron inked across distortions of glass. She called it a second coming, glancing his way, to see if its irreverence amused him. Cordelia and Cecelia, the hooded rat, white and black. The passing of these and every word, word past word.

Reality Made Easy

You've dressed yourself in lavender and green. Fashioned a Boudicca from the cells of your reflection. The moment a form of art becomes invisible. Your gestures an incantation in a wilderness of blood. Those painted ladies. Remember? In Dread County they lifted and lowered their wings. Uncommon disturbances domesticated. You burn them with your voice. Waterbirds whiten the horizon. Small birds fly beneath the surface of the stream. White with its noise. A network of thread entangles our desire. A trailing thread you follow toward your destination. The adolescent frigate bird blown one hundred miles off course. Stranded and bewildered. We breathe now in unison, catalog the weapons of our resilience. Cast our voices into the inarticulate earth and try to speak.

Just a Kiss

Light wired in the trellises. She closed her eyes and walked across a promised land. She opened them. The paper always curled under the sweat of her hand. Here among her marks I found the traces of her body's heat. A dilettante, she took delight in the roots of words. *C'est un collage.* Disparate objects glued together, but also, an affair. He always had a stubborn, no, unyielding mouth. *Décollage.* And she'd started commuting to her marriage again. Through windowless space. Afterward, to her dismay and embarrassment, he broke his silence concerning his recent suicide. Imagine. What dreams are made, unmade of. *Après ça, le mémoire.*

North Beach

I walked up Union
in her perfume
she was wearing
the perfume
noctilucent
clouds and faded

lavender blouse
her fingers
formed rivulets
over the keys
inside a rose
wall with someone

shuffling cards
and erased the left
eyebrow off
an otherwise un-
remarkable face
electronic

bird calls filled
the clouded atrium
she walked across
and through the glass
beyond the fog
dripping through leaves

a diagonal wind
reconciled
the estuary's
intransigence
her substitute
for lucent borders

whatever calculations
she was taught
to regret
in lavender blouse
and faded olive
cotton pants

she walks up Union
soothing
my desire
in her perfume

She fled with the moment

fled the contingencies

off Blackbird Slough

yellow head and red-splotched wing

let their colors rhythm her flight

fled the shiftless hollyhocks

the dog with its distemper

flew beyond the shadow of her dancing

behind a white and floral scrim

fled the busy microbes

their mediations

even the arabesque of her wingless flight

the fragrant air

that circumscribed her memory

of water ice and snow

fled the universal dark

and nameless matter

of which she was herself

an infinitesimal dot

a paradox of her escape

fled innocence the end or mere anatomy

and flew above the cryptic flames

scrawling their code across a lake

The Poet Ponders His Lot

Arthur Rimbaud in my café, talking to himself—his one and only imaginary friend. Obnoxious but cute. A mouse under the table, picking up the poet's crumbs. The mouse speaks English, but squeaks in French. A vector for diseases, that hairless tail, a motor mouth to boot. But cute. Orpheus had his radio, so why must I, the poet mutters, have to take dictation from a rodent? *C'est aussi simple qu'une phrase musicale.* He eyes the mouse. That's easy enough for you to say. If only he could snag a fly on the tip of his tongue, circle the moon, assume the aura circling the moon, describe again *un nid de flammes.* That didn't arrive by radio. The blue in the eyes, a see-through blue. So she walks in, a glimpse of a breast suggesting a course. Then he walks in, his *pantalon* just about to slip his hips. Him or her, the poet thinks, maybe both, I've been around, I'm flexible. Later for the verse. In your dreams, the mouse says, in your dreams, and disappears.

Speed Dating

First kiss, tongue in mouth. You zombie. A tryst with a twist. My sixty seconds in your embrace, you astride your inner horse, dead though it is. Normally, I have to admit, decay is such a deal-breaker. That or politics. But who can afford therapy? I took the pills. So touch me with your lips' remains, let me touch the tattered strands connecting that and that. Work along the borders. There where lightning illuminates our altitudes. Based on base attitudes, of course, my erotic wreck. Can't you now see yourself, despite the weather in your vision, astride your horse, dead though it is, reflected in my desperate eyes?

¿Qué Pasa?

He sent a letter to Venezuela confessing his crime. She wore an anklet of mosquito bites. A piece of broken bathroom tile stuck to his foot. No shower head (it's busted), bedbugs, mildew, dead bugs, must. *Baby, we're goin' dancin' tonight.* They bought a van that Vander built. The Mellow Mushroom. Go on, spoil your bottom. Duck soup, crackers, blood thinner, wine. Had enough of this disaster? Head to Madagascar. Birds can dance, and even camels like to swim. A case for a musical instrument, a small body or body part, an automatic weapon. Under his shirt an oxygen tank. His face a digital composite—tiny photographs of every face he's known. *¿Qué pasa?* What? What's up, man? *Nada.*

FOUR

The reflection in the mirror is always a warning

Big Dog

Various indiscretions spoke of his arrival. Hoist the flag of beautiful contrivances. Though eccentricity's just his cover. His ghost has begun to emerge in the graying of his integuments, the thinning particles of his solidity. He is growing less opaque. Karma, he says, karma and then some. The princess tree spills its royal purple petals onto the walk, but not, he must concede, for him. But resignation's just his cover. Starlight shapes our images, feeds us, soothes us, desiccates and scatters us. The gray Formica splashed with rum. Light flickers along a spider's invisible thread. And yet compulsive observation's just his cover. A praying mantis grips the windshield wiper against his concentration. A passionate embrace. He's reasonable. Though reason too is just another cover.

Semiautomatic

Fictions mend the air. Access and animate his inner contradictions. Semi-automatic. The kick will knock him out of his geometry and into yours. Shot by shot. Arizmendi and sweets before two. Bats filled the air among the conifers. Their dusk bore our fantasies of regeneration. Consumed by the letter blue. Your beauty the tremulous hologram he circled in his need. His nerves have gone all stupid. A standup buffoon, a mystery at noon. Bent from these enduring forms. Semiautomatic. The many parts equal to the whole, though often uninsured. One plus one eleven run. Each bullet displacing, before the report, an indeterminate volume of liquid. Fiber and light.

They Were Gathered

He believed it true but didn't feel its truth. The speaker paused. Laughter. The building rose half-way to the empyrean. A red interior. And buildings don't lie. In the gardens salamanders maneuvered through the leaf mold. Ah, he said. Let it gestate, vegetate. Warm rain softened the air. Instructors spoke three languages at once. Two appeared on a large screen. That seemed to help. *The invisible third almost always strikes a nerve*, they liked to say. Laughter. Succulents continued to grow. Seltzer and plant debris were served at lunch. Trimmings green, serrated, and coarse. Flares lit and dimmed the red interior. Liquor numbed the tongue. Elevators rose to where the sky would be. Words continued to fill the screen. *It's always darkest before the inevitable*. Laughter. T-shirts bearing Firearms Instructor. White lettering on a black ground. *Trust in Allah but tie up your camel*. Pause for laughter, hesitant, osmotic. *Remember, neither sightseeing nor suicide is an option*. Laughter, subdued. Muted cries for reiteration, artificial intelligence, sustainability, romance, hope. They left the hall, went in groups to smaller rooms. Took off their clothes and put on their caps to a song's refrain. Nervous laughter. And there they waited.

Under the Radar

Appendages
were stored
in subterranean jars
along with the assurance
their removal
had been voluntary
and met the current
EPA requirements

Telepathy was sanctioned
though some received
snapshot Xmas cards
displaying ethnic
mutilations
others small boxes
concealing an ear
optic nerve or other
token appendage

Sexual parts were not
contraindicated
even for those
who graphed impermeable
failures of will

Geometry
became a source
of great contentment
though not the algebra

of ecstasy
for those willing to live
in the vicinity
of spiders

Or vamp molecular
improvisations
while plates of shore-fast ice
dissolved and latitude
was magnified

An architect
of surfaces
had superimposed
a gridwork
of planetary
reflections
on curved bands
of invisible sand
and growing
congregations of salt

Uncertainty bled
into the footnotes
and in the coda
laughter was prescribed
for those seized
by the humor of it all

The Dictator Reflects

I have redefined history as hysteria, mirrored in the air

Heavy snows will fall on the orange water of the River X

The name of the great river has been expunged from every text

The definitions of *dioxin* and other Latinate contaminates have been revised in the authoritative lexicon

The gunshots you have heard in the courtyard near the ministry have restored the balance I desire

Those unable to walk on their own are carried to the wall and secured by the wrists

Never embarrassed, your sister let others be embarrassed in her place

I have recalibrated her resistance to stimuli

I have extended the mines in every direction and increased the weight of collateral debris filling the ravines

Shafts of radioactivity penetrate the mountain's core

A perturbation of the heart has become an affliction among the people

I have barricaded the cities and sealed the gates

Scrap metal nested a thousand meters deep continues to orange in the autumn rain

The word *pellagra* is no longer to be spoken in the wards

Others will be posted

I have made the sexual affect an artifact of memory

The reflection in the mirror is always a warning

I have made your brother lower his head and ask for mercy

In the Realm of the Sightless Warriors

Concentric
circles of light
light through vapors
and crystals of ice
sundog

parhelion
in the realm of the sightless warriors

In mere minutes
from sun to here
light burned into the surface
apertures
apertures that almost fit
their fingertips

Before their
depleted eyes
large polyps descended
in a scented room

By touch they recorded
twenty-seven invertebrates
troglodytes
endemic to the thirty caves
they had diagrammed in the granite Canyon
of the Basket Hats

Their instruments detected
coronal eruptions
while microbes digested
their memories of glass

If only they could see
see in their reflections
the knots of pain
numb them in their focused gaze

Spasms bent back
their necks and spines

while thousands
of terra-cotta warriors
made in their image
guarded the gates

where old men in red or purple
garments with insignias
measured the changing
units of time

in the realm
of the sightless warriors

Floating Chrysanthemums

As they fell above the sea
those alien clusters
of suicide planes
those *floating chrysanthemums*
our eyelids
   adrenaline of desire

Fulgura frango
an inscription against the storm
I break up the lightning
Don't we all she said as
the bell tower
   the turbulence
under her skin
   thunder
     the adrenaline

He suffered from a delusion
of parasites
delusory parasitosis
hid in the static
   of his obsessions
suffered the programmed cell death
his injuries   remembered
   combat   now brought on

If someone is worth
shooting once they're worth shooting
         twice they said

Harmonic tremors crossed the ocean floor
replicated the tremors of his desire
         a dull pulsation
at the base of the skull

As they fell to the sea
those miniature exploding suns
         chrysanthemums
a profusion on the membrane
         of our desire

FIVE

Aparatos imaginarios para aprender a decir adiós

—Ulalume González de León
"Inventario," *Plagios*

Rear Projection

For they have sown the wind, and they shall reap the whirlwind . . .
—Hosea 8:7

Those spirits you've called up circulate, drift down between your parted fingers. Grass blades lifting one by one where the hand was.

The kite rose, dipped and soared as Handel's *Water Music* measured currents above the Green.

When her loose gown from her shoulders did fall . . .

An accretion of light against the squat, discolored sycamore, adobe wall, that shadowless figure waiting for a bus.

She passes on the back of a motorcycle, her hair stirring, tinseling the wind. Your long, straight toes and bright red polish.

algorithms, parametrics, kill ratios, our fantasies a whirlwind of sand and blood.

I held your imagined atoms as we crossed the room, the scent of amaretto still on your breath, a trace of sugar on your upper lip. A watermark now visible on an orange paper wing.

He touched the escalator's revolving belt, felt it under his fingers as it slipped away. Has time already lost track of us? In the spinning helix where our bodies and thoughts take rest.

Time Zones

Those scars under the soft cloth
    the phantom
cancer's cryptogram

another
you covered
in red ochre green and blue

Upon its discovery
somewhere in China
they gave it a name

    crowned dragon
of the five-colored rocks

A blue pane floats above
lovers in a darkened room

as winter pine and oak pollen
slid across the fractured rock

The tribes fed on tubers
    bulbs and roots
plotted the inclinations of matter

our fields of solace and sensation

where green ferns layered the slope

and white moths among the white flowers of dusk

Scarred layers of sedimentary language

fireflies and timbered joists

those dunes of unknown material

you stood on one

    of Saturn's moons

Gone

you a composition of desire   even in the fog   star
jasmine burdens the air, its fragrance a devious substitute
yes, even in the fog

take us to your Russia, Natalya   your frozen sun blurring
its migrations of snow, those blue and senseless distances
Natalya   take us from these disappearing surfaces

we've ground the lenses for clarity   *for poetry makes*
nothing happen   yet Spinoza inhaled the powdered glass
of his trade and died of it

have you ever pined for the perfect role   rolled for the
perfect dream   dreamed the perfect mountain   *where the pine its*
garland weaves   woven the perfect sacrificial mountain tree

the moving air moved through your reflection beyond the
window above the walk   the living too moved through
you   I looked right through them to traffic beyond

then one day you began you began to disappear
lingering there behind me   your reflection gone   and if
I turn around one day, you won't be there

El Autobús

past the haze   out there   east of us

    low mountains adrift along a longitude

  of loss   like us, *corazón*   the bus along a narrow strip

        of shoulderless road

21° north latitude

      moist air the sun stirring

          its molecules

La Peñita south toward   an absence   lassitude

    airwaves bearing a lover's   song of lament

una mujer, su niña next to me   where you would be, *corazón*

      that plaintive voice   loss in an other

in comprehensible language   105° west longitude

      location location location   a ghost's lament

  do ghosts, *corazón*,

      pass through one another wordless

        like the rest of us

a narrow strip of blacktop

    threading its coordinates

        degrees seconds minutes hours

the bewitchment of time   *el tiempo engañoso*

    past the haze the mountains

  drifting off   like us, *corazón mio*

Gone Astray

That bird flying into the future left us behind
what hallucinations fill those trees
    gone astray in thought
you wait for a voice under the oak
beyond your expectations
or trace of where you've been
talus stealing the mountain trail
clouds moving their shadows across the slopes
our first language knitted in place
or twined around a vision

    we *amateurs*   *amator*   *amare*

            lover   *to love*

Acknowledgments

Many thanks to the editors of the following publications, in which these poems first appeared, sometimes with different titles:

Aji: "Shostakovich," "Drift Prairie"; *Apollo's Lyre*: "Another Air"; *Blueprint*: "Time Zones"; *CLWN WR*: "the garden," "sea array"; *Digging Our Poetic Roots—Poems from Sonoma County* (WordTemple Press): "Time Zones," "El Autobús"; *Doorknobs & Bodypaint*: "Pluto," "Doctor of Illusion," "The Language of Burial"; *Fault Lines*: "Brief Time"; *Homestead Review*: "For Brendan," "These"; *It's Animal but Merciful* (Great Weather for MEDIA): "Q's world (MIA)," "Q's world (under the mountain)"; *The Medulla Review*: "Days Like This," "Reality Made Easy," "Speed Dating"; *North Coast Literary Review*: "Writing"; *Forgotten*: "Hurricane Coast"; *Otoliths*: "Badlands," "To Persia and the Park Beyond," "*Welt Detektiv*," "Dark Druid of the Sídhe," "Re mem ber?," "The Poet Ponders His Lot"; *PoetsEleven*: "Rear Projection," "They Were Gathered," "The Dictator Reflects"; *riverbabble*: "Cannonball Adderley, Jazz Workshop, 1959," "Woman with Dog"; *San Francisco Peace and Hope*: "the passage"; *War*: "Floating Chrysanthemums"; *you say. say.* (Uphook Press): "I Don't Know What," "Weather Report."

"For Brendan" and "These" won the Central Coast Writers First Place Poetry Awards.

I want to express my gratitude to the members of Sixteen Rivers Press for their encouragement and support.

Notes

"Cauchemar": French for *nightmare*.

"Cannonball Adderley, Jazz Workshop, 1959": While in San Francisco, Dmitri Shostakovich attended this performance.

"For Brendan": St. Brendan's legendary journey to the Isle of the Saints appears in the medieval Latin narrative *Navigatio Sancti Brendani Abbatis*.

"Weather Report": The quotation is from Cormac McCarthy's *The Road*. The image of the dolphin evolved out of a conversation with Jon Campo.

"Drift Prairie": Coteau des Prairies is a glacial plateau in eastern South Dakota.

"Badlands": Miles Davis composed "So What"; Thelonious Monk, "Well You Needn't"; and Bill Evans, "Peace Piece." *Les mauvaises terres à traverser* is the French name for the Badlands, *mako sica*, the Lakota name.

"Dark Druid of the Sídhe": The Sídhe, pronounced *she*, is the home of a supernatural race in Irish mythology.

"Pluto": "She-lion woman" is a variation on "Sea Lion Woman," the title of an African American folk song that Herbert Halpert recorded on a trip to the South in 1939 with singers Katherine and Christine Shipp. It can be found at the Library of Congress.

"Q's world (MIA)" and "Q's world (under the mountain)": After conversations with Q, an acquaintance who spends time in another world.

"Reality Made Easy": After the rape of her daughters, the Celtic queen Boudicca led an uprising against the Romans and burned Roman London. The painted lady is a species of butterfly.

"The Poet Ponders His Lot": This Orpheus appears in the films of Jean Cocteau's *Orphic Trilogy*. *C'est aussi simple qu'une phrase musicale* ("It's as simple as a musical phrase") is from Rimbaud's *Guerre (War)*; *un nid de flammes* ("a nest of flames") is from his *Une Saison en Enfer (A Season in Hell)*.

"In the Realm of the Sightless Warriors": I am indebted to two works of art: The description of light is from Charles Ross's *8 Minutes, 19 Seconds*; the description of polyps from Ernesto Neto's *Léviathan Thot*. The Chinese terra-cotta figures date from the third century BCE.

Epigraph: "Imaginary devices for learning to say goodbye," "Inventory," *Plagiarisms*. Translation by Nancy J. Morales, Terry Ehret, and John Johnson.

"Rear Projection": The quotation is from Thomas Wyatt's "They Flee from Me." The line that begins "*algorithms . . .*" is italicized for emphasis.

"Time Zones": The quotation "our fields . . ." comes from Edgar Wayburn's *Your Land and Mine: Evolution of a Conservationist*.

"Gone": The first quotation is from W. H. Auden's "In Memory of W. B. Yeats," the second from Percy Bysshe Shelley's "To Jane: The Invitation."

"*El Autobús*": Thanks to Suyapa Escobar for her reading of the poem and her comments.